Drawing Down Belial

Ψ

S. Connolly

Drawing Down Belial

Daemonic Divination, Ascension, and Channeling

Ψ

S. Connolly

DB PUBLISHING 2014

MMXIV

DB Publishing is an arm of Darkerwood Publishing Group, PO Box 2011, Arvada, CO 80001.

ISBN: 978-1-312-23557-1

Drawing Down Belial © 2014 by S. Connolly. No part of this book may be reproduced in any form, electronic or other, without express written permission from the author and publisher. Buy only authorized electronic copies. Please respect the author's copyright.

Book Design by Kim Anderson
Editor: T. Jenkins
Cover Art by Prism

For Trish and Paimon. Thank you both for the limitless inspiration.

ACKNOWLEDGEMENTS

A special thank you to Tanya. Thanks for standing by me during this project and offering such valuable input. You are truly a talented seeress and sorceress, and I'm honored to call you friend and a sister in the artes. I'd also like to thank Andrieh Vitimus for sending Paimon along to give me a swift kick in the ass. Props to you, my friend!

Table of Contents

Author's Foreword	1
A Brief Introduction to Daemonic Divination, Ascension & Channeling	5
Preparation of the Seer/Medium	11
Spirit Boards	16
Pendulums (Dowsing)	24
Scrying	34
Reading Daemonic Sigils	51
Tarot	53
Channeling	59
Ascension	66
Dream Divination & Communication	72
The Rituals of Divination	75
Additional Daemonic Commentary	85
Resources & Reading	88

Author's Foreword

Back in 2000 I had a series of interesting discussions with an old friend about divination, ascension practice and channeling the Daemonic Divine. We discussed the varied and wondrous pathwork that such ascension produced, and came up with the idea of writing a book aided by channeled Daemons. My friend, who'd heard my tales of *The Shadow Leviathan* and their Belial channeling sessions, and who was a dedicant and priestess to Belial, suggested it be called *Drawing Down Belial*. Sadly, she died unexpectedly in 2006 at the young age of thirty-four. At the time of her death we were at odds with one another (bitter enemies some would say). A fated prophesy by a psychic medium warned me back in 1999 that my friend and I would suffer a fate similar to Crowley and Mathers. Our friendship did, indeed, suffer. But after her death I was able, with help from a non-involved necromantic sorceress and Daemonolatress, to reconcile with my friend posthumously.

In the years that followed I would be driving to work or minding my own business when I'd hear the haunting words *Drawing Down Belial*. Finally, in April of 2012 she wouldn't take no for an answer and so I promised I would write this book. It was a brilliant idea really, but like all work, sometimes it takes time to percolate, and it's written when it's ready to be written. This book was ready to be written with much thanks to Paimon, and my friend Andrieh, who sent Paimon over.

Ask those who enlist my channeling abilities to speak with the Daemonic divine and I think you'll find the overwhelming response is positive. I am one of those rare folks who took to channeling Daemons like a fish takes to water. So when I presented this idea to my Patron, he was very eager to get started as were other Daemons who stepped up at the chance to be part of a book about Daemonolatry divination.

First I'd like to point out that some of this information was already printed in *The Daemonolater's Guide to Daemonic Magick*. However, A LOT has been added. My thinking behind this book was that some folks out there are specifically into Divination and would like their own manual as well as exercises and further commentary on what I had to say on the matter. Daemonic Divination is a topic that is often misunderstood, and the short sections in *Daemonolater's Guide to Daemonic Magick* (DGDM) amounted to about twenty-two pages of material. This book, clearly, exceeds twenty pages. That book didn't allow for me to get into the fine details of the divinatory arts. This one does and it gives the Daemonic an opportunity to directly address the magi who would choose to practice the divinatory arts with the aid of the Daemonic.

I'll do my best to not wax poetic at you, however when you begin working with Daemons to help one write a book, sometimes their archaic usage and riddles sound rather poetic. I, for the most part, am rather up front in my writing. Daemons, on the other hand, are not. Writing this book has been a rather sobering and enlightening experience for me, so hopefully you'll find it useful and inspirational to your own practice.

So what does this book include that Daemonolater's Guide to Daemonic Magick didn't aside from Daemonic input? Well, we will discuss both blood scrying and fire scrying in this book, for one. We'll also discuss pendulum usage since it's the most versatile form of divination and the easiest, most accessible, form of divination. Even people who have no mediumship skills can pick up dowsing. Not to mention you can do it anywhere with little to no set-up.

Finally, this book contains the commentary, tips, tricks, and discussion missing in *DGDM*, about using these divination devices in conjunction with the Daemonic to amplify the divination session and give the magus clear focus and strong, clear messages. This book also gives exercises and suggests meditations and various workings to help build and hone your divination skills. I've done my best to be more thorough here and really dig in to the subject matter – bringing you a highly practical and accessible manual of Daemonolatry divination sans too much hand-holding. Remember that to truly learn and understand it's best to jump right in. Don't worry too much about doing it wrong because you can fix any mistake you make.

This book will be used as the standard textbook in all of the divination classes and workshops I teach. So, if you are looking to get some personal feedback and help with your divination practice, do make sure to sign up for one of my online workshops where I will work personally with you to help you hone your divinatory skills.

Remember that the best way to hone any skill is to practice, practice, practice. When I was sixteen and just learning tarot, I would read for just about anyone who asked. When I had no one to read for, I read for myself. I even read for family pets and the pets of friends. So grab Fido or Fluffy and read for them if you need practice and are tired of reading for yourself.

With that – let us begin!

S. Connolly
January 2014

A Brief Introduction to Daemonic Divination, Ascension & Channeling

Divination is how one foretells the future or discovers answers to the hidden or mysterious by means of communicating with a spirit or entity or the higher self. Daemons are not a necessary part of this equation, but since this book is geared toward Daemonolaters, we are discussing Daemonic divination. There are many methods for divination.

The most common methods among Daemonic Magicians are:

- Specially Prepared Spirit Boards (i.e. Ouija)
- Dowsing with the use of Pendulums
- Scrying Mirrors/Crystals/Bowls/Fire/Blood
- Reading Daemonic Sigils
- Tarot Cards
- Channeling (Includes Automatic Writing)
- Ascension (Astral Work)
- Dream Divination

Admittedly most forms of divination require the person performing the divination to be a medium of some sort. If you're not – don't worry, there is a place for you with the pendulum. There are four main types of mediumship ability and most mediums will have one to four of these abilities depending on sensitivity. Some will add smell (*Clairalience*) and taste (*Clairgustance*) to this list, but I tend to throw those under the Clairsentience umbrella, despite the fact I probably shouldn't.

The first is **clairsentience**, *clear knowing* or *to know*. That is – a medium who just knows things. This ability can actually be broken down into two because some Clairsentient mediums can foretell the future and others cannot. So the first type of medium is the clairsentient who simply knows things and can translate what they 'know' into words. Intuition is a clairsentient ability and is actually quite common. It's learning to listen to that inner voice that most people struggle with. The second type of clairsentient is one that knows what is going to happen (in the future). The third type of medium is the **clairvoyant**, *clear sight* or *to see*. Clairvoyants pick up things from objects, places, others, and situations as images. So clairvoyance means the medium's mind gives them images that the medium must translate into coherent thoughts. This can be easier said than done. It can take some practice depending on the level of natural ability. The last type of medium is someone who experiences **clairaudience**, *clear hearing* or *to hear*. That is – they "hear" whatever it is they're picking up. Not in a psychotic, schizophrenic hearing voices kind of way, but rather they 'hear' whatever they're picking up in their mind. So his or her internal voice may say something like, "Someone died here." Whereas a Clairsentient would just know, in their gut, that someone had died, and someone with Clairvoyance might actually get a vision of the deceased. Some mediums might get a combination of all three.

Divination can actually be used in magick to, for example, communicate with the Daemonic to learn how to perform certain magicks. Or, to discover if magick has or will manifest. Divination can also be the part of the magickal process of invoking the Daemonic entity. Or, magick can be used to make a divination session more productive. Ultimately – you use divination to learn about the unknown or the future of any situation. You, as one who practices the divinatory arts with the aid of Daemons, utilize Daemonic forces to heighten this ability of knowing or uncovering that information that is hidden.

Of course just because you're working with Daemons doesn't mean you're going to suddenly have powers of divination or ascension/channeling bestowed upon you overnight. Natural ability varies from person to person. You'll still have to hone these skills and honing magickal skills can take years. So please don't get discouraged if you're not getting the results you want after a few tries. I can't begin to tell you how many people I've encountered over the years who expect to have powerful divination or channeling skills after a few tries.

In my book *Keys of Ocat*, I discussed at some length the reason some people may have difficulty learning certain types of divination. In that book, obviously, it was about communicating with the dead rather than the Daemonic, but it still applies to all divination and spirit communication skills. I think it's rather important for anyone seeking to learn divination and communication, or hone their existing skills, to learn what type of medium one is.

Here is my handy-dandy chart explaining the types of divination that work best for the type of ability the magician naturally has:

- **Clairsentient:** Pendulum, Spirit Boards
- **Clairvoyant:** Crystal Balls, Scrying Bowls, Scrying Mirrors, Fire Scrying
- **Clairaudient:** Pendulum, Spirit Boards

So, from knowing what type of medium you are, start with a divination device that is more apt to work with your particular skillset. If you're one of the lucky magicians who has a natural aptitude for all of them, then just choose the divination device you are most attracted to.

If you're still experiencing difficulty getting results, there are other factors you can consider. One factor that can weigh in on success is the magician's elemental alignment. Earthy people are more likely to "ground" their abilities whereas air people may experience an inability to focus. The goal of earthy folks should be to learn to let go without grounding (even when attending a session where someone else is doing the divination or channeling – you might inadvertently ground the efforts of other mediums!). Air people should practice keeping focus if they find themselves losing contact easily. Fire people may find themselves able to draw spirits with ease, but may find communication difficult because they so intently focus on the sensation of connecting. The goal here is to learn to let go of the feeling, and focus instead on the communication. Water people are the most psychic of all the elements and the biggest downfall here seems to be fear. If a water person cannot scry it's more likely because they're terrified of what they see in the mirror, not that they can't see into the mirror. The goal here is to remember that you are in control. Daemons are not going to hurt you. Now if you're working with the dead, that's another story. For advice on the necromantic arts, I do recommend you pick up *Keys of Ocat*, which discusses necromancy in great detail.

Finally, one of the biggest factors in the success of divination, channeling and ascension practices is mindset. What is your mindset? Are you a definite skeptic? Are you secretly afraid to make contact? These mindsets can make or break a session. You may not be open to making contact if you really do fear the Daemonic or the dead or have other attitudes that would hinder your progress. If you have confidence for contact and no fear – you're more likely to make contact. If you are full of doubt and fear – you won't. The law of attraction applies.

Lastly, let's discuss expectations. Yes – some people can contact the Daemonic or perform divination and get strong, clear messages rather easily. Try dropping all expectations of your own gifts if you're just starting out. Let them develop naturally without comparing yourself to other people with gifts. Your gift is always going to be different from the next person's. You may be able to channel a Daemon with no problem, but maybe spirit boards just don't work for you. Don't worry about it. Remember that divination devices are merely tools to an end goal. You may be someone who always needs the tool, or you may be one of those lucky individual who doesn't need tools. Or who will use the tool to start, but will fully connect without needing the tool for the rest of the session. You're not in competition with others. Your end goal is the same – to communicate with the Daemonic and get answers.

There are a few things you probably need to know to use this book. The first is that **I am assuming you**

already know something of Daemonolatry. That is, Daemon worship. Ultimately it means working with Daemons in a respectful manner and treating them like the divine intelligences they are. I also assume that you know **an enn is an invocation from the Daemonic language**. You can get Daemonolatry based enns from a book I refer to a lot in this book – the *Daemonolater's Guide to Daemonic Magick (DGDM)*. Or you can get them for free online at http://www.demonolatry.org/ in the files and downloads section. Many enns can also be found in *The Complete Book of Demonolatry*. If you do not want to use enns – feel free to formulate your own invocations. This is perfectly acceptable. I may also refer to recipes that can be found in the next section of the book, or recipes that can be found in DGDM. Finally, I assume you know how to find sigils for various spirits. The aforementioned website contains numerous Daemonic seals (Daemonolatry specific) and you can find all Goetic seals looking at any copy of the goetia, or with a quick online search. I'm not going to repeat all of that here.

Now onto the various methods of divination useful for the magician to, in the very least, know about. If you have tried many of these methods and failed with them, or if you are not sure of your mediumship ability, choose the pendulum to work with first. Most people have, in the very least, some mild abilities, usually in the form of Clairsentience (intuition).

Preparation of the Seer/Medium

We all have our own ways to prepare for divination. For some, we pour ourselves a cup of coffee, don our favorite pair of slippers, and settle down in a comfortable chair. For others they may meditate or do yoga beforehand. No matter what you do, I recommend a few standard steps.

First, drink enough water. Second, if you are using a divination tea – prepare and drink it. Third, if you are using tinctures to help you get where you want to go, take them. Fourth, if you are using a balm or flying ointment – apply it to your pulse points and/or third eye. Finally, make yourself and your surroundings as comfortable as possible for you, your clients or friends, and most importantly the spirits or Daemons you may be working with (if any). Remember that divination doesn't need to involve spirits, but since I am writing this book about connecting and divining via Daemons, that's the perspective you're getting here. Theoretically you can nix any and all spirit communication and simply connect with your higher self. So keep that in mind as you read.

Next, here is a recipe for a basic divination oil/oleum that you can use to anoint all of your divination devices before use.

Basic Divination Oleum:

In ½ cup of olive oil, macerate two sprigs of fresh Wormwood (if dried, 1 teaspoon) and two tablespoons of mugwort. You can heat it gently to allow the herbal essence to infuse with the oil, or simply allow it to steep for several weeks in a cool, dark place. Strain, add four drops of tincture of benzoin (to preserve and enhance) or just vodka (to preserve) and bottle in amber bottles for use.

Now on to other recipes. So I've talked about all these tinctures and teas and ointments to help you out. I might as well provide some recipes for you. You will find recipes for scrying waters and divination incenses in the scrying section of the book. Everything else is here.

Flying Ointment

There are many recipes for traditional flying ointments out there. They can be used during any divination session and should be used with caution due to often highly toxic (i.e. poisonous) ingredients. This is my favorite recipe by far.

In 1/4 cup of melted beeswax add a pinch of fresh, dried and powdered mandrake root, a pinch of dried and powdered belladonna leaves, a pinch of powdered, dried hops, five drops of clary sage oil, and a pinch of powdered calamus root. Let the heat extract the herbal essences and infuse with the beeswax. Pour into small containers and allow to cool. Then cap and use as needed. You can use mandrake and belladonna tinctures or oils (three to five drops each) in this recipe instead of the plant matter.

How is it applied? Some people apply the ointment to the third eye or the pulse points. Others will apply it under the nose. I personally use a method where a tiny amount is applied in the nostril, directly to the mucus membrane. However, I DO NOT advise others to do this because it could trigger an allergic reaction. Experiment at your own risk. Please note that these are toxic substances and if you have allergies or you use too much, this flying ointment can make you very sick. It should not be used daily. I recommend folks start by applying it to their pulse points in small amounts and increase as needed. See how your body reacts to the ointment first.

Divination Tinctures

Please note that these tinctures are all either poisonous or illegal. I only include them for reference. Use them at your own risk.

Tincture of Mandrake - for Ascension Practice (POISONOUS)

This can be made one of two ways. The first is to take a mandrake root, score it, and macerate it in a jar of vodka forever, using it as needed. Keep it in a cool, dark place. The second method is to fill a beaker with distilled water. Add fresh leaves from the mandrake plant (crush them to release their essence) into the water. Each week, add new leaves and new water - not removing the old water or old leaves. Do this for a month. This is an extraction of mandrake essence by method of putrefaction. Once the month has passed, the putrefied mandrake essence water is strained of all plant matter. It should smell awful. This liquid is then added to the vodka directly. You can add a scored mandrake root to the liquid after that and then store it in a cool, dark place and use as needed. I recommend 5 drops sub lingually (under the tongue) to start before any channeling or ascension session.

Tincture of Wormwood - for general Divination and Communication (TOXIC IN LARGE DOSES)

For tincture of wormwood I will often add a cup of wormwood to two or three cups of vodka and let it steep for at least a month before use, rotating the jar (to mix) once a week. The herbal matter can then be drained off and the tincture can be used 3-5 drops under the tongue (to start) before any divination or communication session.

Tincture of Salvia (Divinorum) - for Ascension Practice (ILLEGAL)

Please note that salvia divinorum is illegal in most states nowadays due to stupid kids using it to get high. This particular plant has been used by shamans for centuries during divination and spiritual work. If you can get it, add a half gram of 20x or 30x Salvia Divinorum to two ounces of rum or vodka. Let it steep for at least two weeks. Then use it a few drops under the tongue at a time. You can increase the number of drops as you go. I don't recommend more than 10-15 drops per session. Remember that the goal of the tincture is to help you get over those inhibitions holding you back from allowing the connection to the Daemonic force. Not to get high.

Divination Teas

Hibiscus Diviner's Tea - Four dried hibiscus flowers, crushed. One teaspoon dried and crushed rosehips. A pinch of cinnamon. 1/4 cup chamomile. Add this to some cheesecloth or a tea ball and steep in 1-2 cups of hot water. Drink before a divination session.

Chervil Tea (to aid in sciomancy and other communication): Take one sprig of fresh Chervil and steep along with a pinch of all three Rosemary, Sage, and Thyme, along with four hibiscus flowers, a dash of cinnamon, and a couple of rosehips. Steep the herbs in hot water, allow the tea to cool, and drink before divination sessions.

Spirit Boards

With Spirit Boards there is a very specific method of preparation that must be followed if you are going to get Daemonic entities ONLY to come through the board. Otherwise you open the board to anything that wishes to communicate with you and that can turn out really bad. I realize that most people reading this will be surprised to learn that even Daemon Worshipers have a deep respect for the proper use of the spirit board and that we'd warn the practitioner at all about them. I assure you this warning comes from personal experience. Boards like the *Ouija* (made by Parker Brothers) are NOT TOYS. As a matter of fact, I wish they'd quit selling the damn things at Toys R Us. All it takes is one board and a real medium – and the boards can become very dangerous. Sure – thousands of people use the boards with no ill effects at all. The key component is a medium. Once you put a medium on the board – every "thing" from the other side is going to see that portal open and whoever or whatever gets there first can attach itself to the board. Sometimes that "whatever" is very bad.

In the *Daemonolater's Guide to Daemonic Magick,* in the chapter covering spirit boards, I shared the story of Samuel and how a friend and I had to learn how to remove a bad spirit from a board because it had turned into a full fledge haunting. These things really do happen if you're not careful. I won't repeat the story here. If you own Daemonolater's Guide to Daemonic Magick you can read it for yourself. However, I will repeat the method of getting rid of nasty spirits from a bad board later in this chapter because it's important people know how to deal with such things and I learned firsthand how difficult it is to find information on how to remove a nasty board replete with spirit from one's life.

Of course this is why it is of the utmost importance that for Daemonic Divination work you use a new board that has never been used and **prepare it first**. You'll be using this board to speak with Daemons only.

Board Preparation

I learned how to do this from my teacher and it's been such a successful method of preparation that I have passed it on to others. This method of prepping a board will exclude everything but Daemons. You might just want to keep two separate boards.

(Doesn't matter if your board is Parker Brothers or not) You have to prep the planchette.

- Delepitore or Azlyn/Azyn Oleum OR Sage oil (See *Wortcunning for Daemonolatry* for *DGDM* for recipes.)
- 1 candle, color of your choice. I always choose a power color – red or purple.
- 1 small stone your choice (think - fits on head of pin). I recommend tiger's eye because it's an energy conduit. Some people prefer quartz.

Generally this is done inside an elemental circle by witness of Satan (or your All), Delepitoré (or equivalent), and/or Azlyn (or equivalent). Any Daemons of divination will work. A lot of people choose Ashtaroth for this purpose, too.

First you anoint the board and the planchette with the oil. Then, you drip candle wax on the planchette to cover it (NOT the indicator window). The sigil of a Daemon of your choice is carved into the wax or drawn on the planchette with oleum. The planchette is anointed again. The stone is affixed, with a tiny dab of glue, at the center of the indicator window (this is why it must be small). You can burn temple incense during this process if you like. I've also glued the stone in the middle of the planchette.

If you do it right - nothing but Daemons will come through the board.

Mind you this will not necessarily make a board work for you. You either have mediumship ability with a board or you don't. This just ensures that nothing but Daemons come through a particular board.

If you don't have a board, you can create a makeshift spirit board with nothing more than some paper, a pen, tape, a table or smooth floor, and a small clear glass. The method is that you draw letters, numbers, and yes/no on the papers, arrange them in a circle on the table or floor (secured with tape). The glass is turned upside down in the center of the circle and that is used as the planchette. To prepare a board like this, anoint the glass with the oil, draw the sigil of a Daemon of divination in the center of table using chalk or crayon, or draw the sigil very small on the corner of each letter/number etc... This method also allows you to create other divination set-ups. For example – your "letters" could be sigils or even complete ideas. For example, if you're looking to decide which project to work on, you could write all of the projects on different papers and whichever one the planchette moves to, there you go. Of course a pendulum might be a faster, more efficient method there. The choice is entirely yours.

Another wonderful thing about this particular set-up is this --- you can put this on a floor or table (or even paint it), then cover it with a table cloth or rug and no one will ever know it's even there. This is rather handy for folks who live in small spaces, or those folks who may not be "out" with regard to their practices.

Now – how to destroy a board that hasn't been prepped and has something nasty attached to it. The first thing is to identify that there is something nasty attached to the board. You'll know. I have no doubt you'll know. If it's a board – it has to be destroyed. Burn the board and planchette, collect the ashes, separate the ashes into two or three separate containers, and distribute those ashes into separate bodies of running water. If you used pieces of paper taped to a floor or table and a glass, remove the paper, burn it, break the glass, collect the broken glass and ashes, separate them into several separate piles and distribute them into separate bodies of running water. If you don't want to pollute a river with glass, you can throw it away in the trash, but I recommend a trash receptacle away from your home. Then you want to clean the table or floor where the letters were taped. Use vinegar, with tincture of benzoin to wash the area, and then clear the house by burning white sage or frankincense. You may even choose to perform a formal banishing ritual. If your spirit board was painted on a table or floor, remove it with paint thinner (or sand it off), then wash it with the vinegar and tincture of benzoin, let it dry, burn the sage or frankincense, then re-stain (or re-wax the floor). Again, use a formal banishing – especially if the paranormal activity was strong. Sometimes, with tables, it's best to get rid of them – especially if simply cleaning them doesn't work.

Using the Board

In many ways, using a spirit board requires someone who can channel. So one of the primary ingredients necessary to use a board correctly is you need someone who is a medium. That means – someone who is sensitive to otherworldly entities and with whom the entities can effectively communicate. Some people – by their mere presence – stilt the flow of energies making communication impossible. The medium(s) and the medium(s) ONLY should place up to three fingers on the planchette. Yes, this means that ONE person can work a board by him/her-self. If the medium senses that anyone in the room is blocking him/her, she should ask that person to leave. A block feels like someone holding you back when you're trying to walk forward. You know that feeling? If you feel that – stop, find the block and remove it.

Ask for the Daemonic entity you would like to speak with and the planchette should start moving. I get figure eights, others get circles. Then you begin asking questions. Keep a pad of paper and pen ready (someone else to record the session is ideal). When you have made contact you will feel a feathery, electricity sensation through the top of your hands and through your fingers and you'll also feel a strange energy "pressure" move evenly through your fingers. Your fingers are still resting lightly on the planchette. You may feel that electricity feeling up through your wrists (it almost tickles). It's not an unpleasant sensation, just strange at first. It's quite normal. You may need to shake out your hands in the middle of a session or afterward. Remember that using a board is one step removed from channeling! You are literally drawing the Daemonic energy through your hands.

The Daemonic force or entity responds to each question by moving the planchette from letter to letter to spell out words. More sensitive mediums may also find they get images and/ or actually "hear" in their mind's eye the words before they're finished being spelled out. And when they think the words, the planchette will jump to yes. If you are this type of medium your sessions will be much more productive. Expect that your medium (or you if you're the medium) will be tired after long durations of board work. It's the nature of the beast. Again – it is almost channeling – just like Ascension practice. This can make spirit boards more difficult to work with, especially if a person harbors fear of channeling – that sensation of being 'taken over'. Not everyone can deal with that because they fear losing control. Consider this as a possible stumbling block if you're having a hard time getting the board to work for you.

Spirit Board Exercise:

An exercise suggestion to help you hone your ability is this: Alone, within a Daemonically charged circle if you find it necessary (more advanced practitioners may not need this balance, beginners do), set the board in front of you. Place your forefinger and middle finger of both hands on the planchette. Move it around a few times. You'll notice the pressure you place on the board moving it around on your own with no spirit interaction whatsoever. Now close your eyes and concentrate on a Daemonic spirit, take a deep breath, and submerge yourself in the feeling of energy running through your hands. Repeat the Daemon's enn under your breath (if you don't know how to use Enn Invocations, I recommend reading *The Complete Book of Demonolatry*). Now relax and focus on letting go. At this point you may find the planchette moving. Don't stop it. Let it move, just focus on the sensation and connection with the Daemonic. If you feel comfortable, just look down and see what is being spelled out to you. Focusing on feelings will help you learn the difference between YOU and the connection with the Daemonic. So the key in the exercise is to not worry so much about the communication at first – but to the connection you're getting. The connection is important because it facilitates the communication.

This exercise can be used in conjunction with various energy work exercises, which also teach us how to differentiate between our own energy fields and those of spirits and/or Daemons. It's obviously a handy exercise for those learning how to channel, too. See the channeling section for more exercises.

TIPS

1. Make sure you are comfortable and relaxed.
2. If you are getting odd messages that don't seem to be anything, write them down anyway.
3. Remember that Daemonic communication isn't always straight forward or direct. Sometimes what the Daemon is trying to say and what you're hearing are two different things. If the literal interpretation (on your part) isn't working, try not taking the message so literally and look for an alternative, metaphoric interpretation. For example: Let's say you ask a Daemon about your relationship woes and the Daemon tells you, "You are going to die." First – who isn't, but secondly, it's probably not meant literally. It's likely meant as, "You will be devastated by the heartbreak of a breakup and your trust for others will be compromised and your ability to love as freely in the future stifled." If you are getting a literal message, it's usually accompanied by a strong ping of intuition telling you it's dead on.
4. Take your time with the messages, don't rush, and keep your mind quiet so you can listen. This is one of the most important things for a medium/seer to learn. Listen.

Ashtaroth Adds: *The differences in the current are rather subtle, therefore one must be vigilant in learning to meditate in their splendor while immersed within their glory. This can be accomplished within the vast caverns of the intellect being always aware of the blending of the physical and subtle bodies. That gray area where light and darkness converge within.*

Pendulums (Dowsing)

Using a pendulum is called "Dowsing". Pendulums really don't require preparation for use but I always recommend they be consecrated and anointed with a Daemonic oleum (oil) before use. If you are new to working with Daemons and you want to make sure you are communicating with a Daemonic entity, use the pendulum in a constructed elemental space as prescribed in *The Complete Book of Demonolatry*. That will often keep unwanted visitors out. Pendulums can also be used, like all divination devices, to communicate with your subconscious, higher self.

Pendulums can be made of different materials and require regular cleansing. I recommend having pendulums made from different materials to communicate with different entities. I use emerald to communicate with earthy Daemons, tiger's eye for Fire Daemons, turquoise or amethyst for water Daemons, and quartz for air Daemons. Your personal preferences may differ from mine. I merely include my preferences to spark your imagination and give you inspirational examples to encourage experimentation.

Since I often use stone pendulums, I regularly leave them in a bowl of salt, wash them off, run them through incense smoke and let them dry naturally. I will re-anoint them with a divination oil (see the Preparation of the Seer/Medium chapter or *Daemonolater's Guide to Daemonic Magick* or *Wortcunning for Daemonolatry*) after each cleansing. I also anoint my third eye with a camphor based salve, like **Tiger Balm** (a tip I was given by my teacher and have given all of my students since the late 90's), before each divination session. You can use that tip for ANY type of divination, ascension or channeling. The reason behind this is that camphor stimulates awareness of the physical and spiritual, making the bridge that much more evident during a session. I always keep a small bottle of the **red Tiger Balm** in my ritual space because of this. You can get it at your local pharmacy. It has camphor in it. Please don't get it in your eyes.

Let's briefly discuss use of the pendulum. Hold your pendulum by the chain or string between your thumb and forefinger:

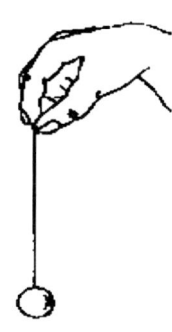

Alternatively, you can slip the bead/ball usually at the end of the pendulum between your forefinger and middle finger, letting the pendulum hang freely. You hold your hand horizontally level. I suggest keeping your elbow on a flat surface to help keep your hand steady at first until you get the hang of a steady hand.

To use the device, ask questions and whichever way the pendulum swings, that's your answer. For some people a counterclockwise swing means no, and a clockwise swing means yes. For others, a pendulum that swings left to right is yes and to and fro means no whereas a circular swing means nothing. You can either decide which works best for you, or ask the Daemonic energies (or what or whomever you are communicating with) to show you yes or no (repeat for clarity).

Now – that above is the "short" version of how to properly dowse. Let's take a moment to talk about baseline questioning. A lot of people concern themselves with spirits being liars. Daemons notoriously have this reputation, obviously colored by those who practice Judeo-Christian magick.

Ashtaroth had this to say about Daemons and lying: *What use is the mind if it cannot think for itself, nor find solace in its own counsel? Sometimes a mistruth is in lack of trust and sometimes it speaks volumes of the magus in question. A clue to the harsh realities facing his journey forward, or a response to inspire independent thought and reason because the Daemonic cannot be relied on for all things lest one becomes dependent and unable to function as a physical being. We are not corporeal. Dependency can be a problem between the mortal and spirit worlds.*

First – when you first begin dowsing, you'll want to ask baseline questions to see if the spirit is with you. Some people will ask questions like, "Is the sky blue?" "Is my boyfriend Bob?" The problem I see with this is some Daemons are snarkier than others. Lucifer might tell you that "No, the sky isn't blue. What you see is a refraction of light making you think the sky is blue." Of course with a pendulum you can, theoretically only get specific answers and if those answers are yes/no – you're just getting a no, with no additional information. This is the drawback of pendulums, but it is also the beauty of pendulums!

This is where nifty pendulum charts, that you can make yourself, come in. You can use a spirit board, sigils and runes, and tarot with a pendulum, or you can simply use charts. There are so many possibilities for pendulum use that really, the sky is the limit. The pendulum will swing toward the answer whether you're asking which way to go, or which tarot card you should meditate on. Or which Daemonic sigil to use, for that matter. You simply place the pendulum over the choices, ask your question, it begins swinging – and there you go. People use pendulums to ask everything from which color suits me to will it rain tomorrow. People will also use them to find lost things. Just ask the question and head in the direction the pendulum swings.

For whatever reason, pendulums are just more accessible to more people, mediums or not. This method of divination can be easily learned. On the following pages are some ideas for pendulum charts that you can make yourself with a pen and piece of paper. If you're really creative, draw them on nice pieces of cardboard or wood, and you can keep them for future use. You can always make new ones as needed. Enjoy!

Yes/ No Chart Samples

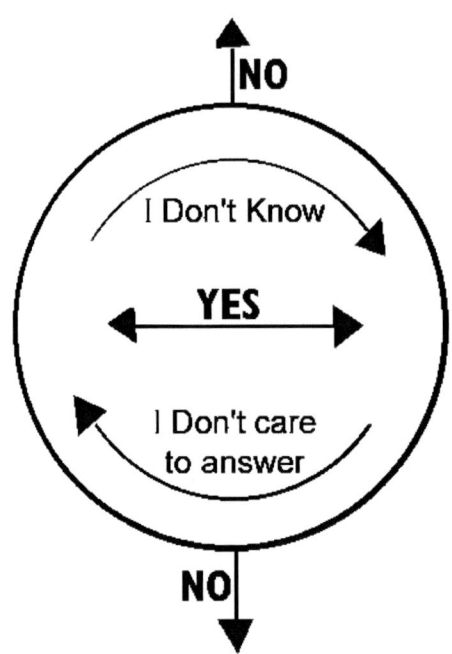

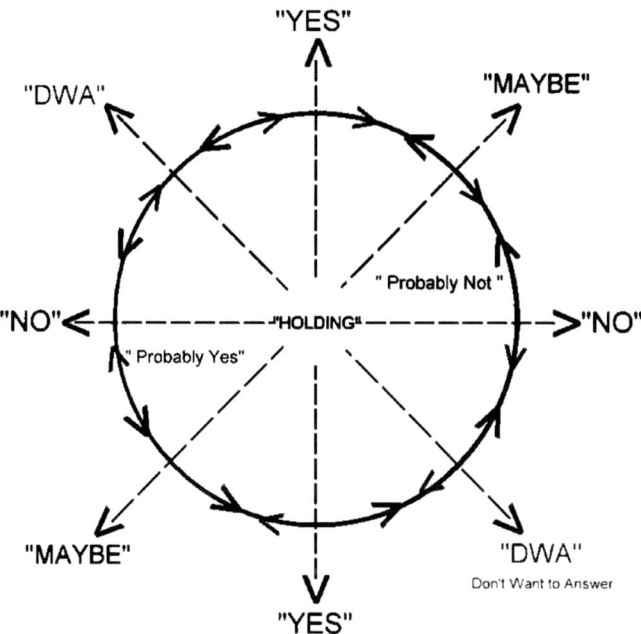

More Charts for Inspiration

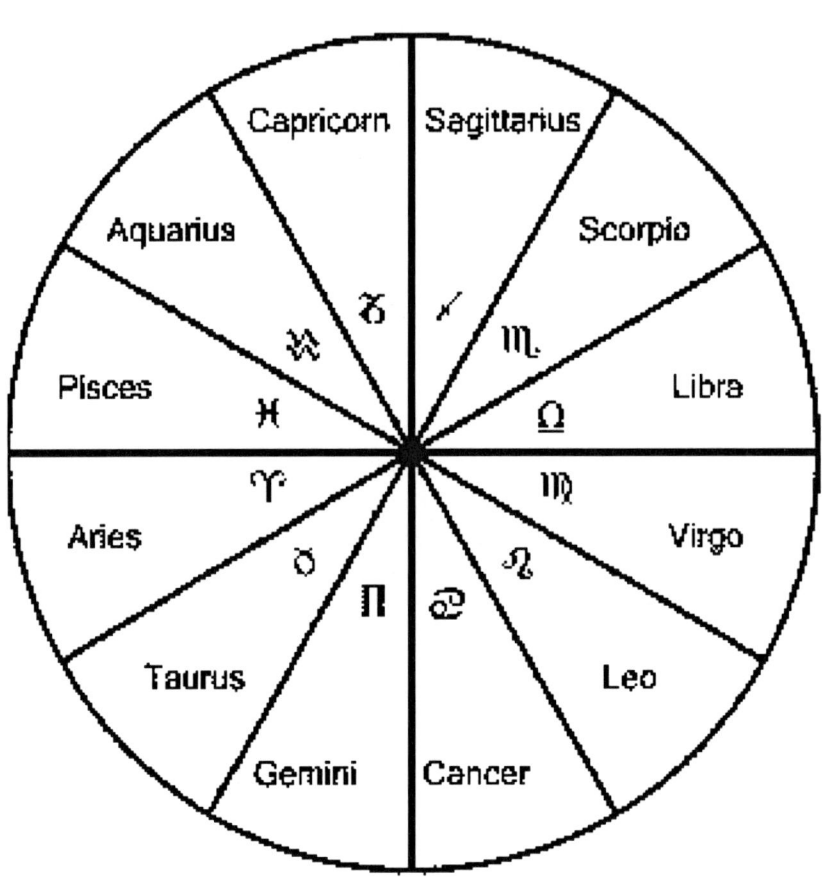

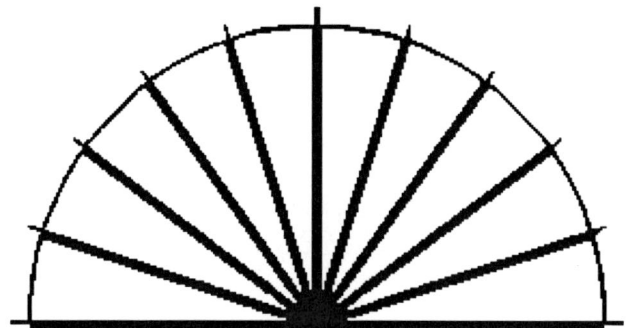

Pendulum Exercise:

Holding the pendulum over a yes/no chart, keep your hand steady, close your eyes, relax, and concentrate on the Daemon you're attempting to contact. Repeat the Daemon's enn as necessary. Chanting or vibrating the enn works rather well during this. Feel the Daemon's energy surround you. Feel it in your hand holding the pendulum.

Now open your eyes and observe the swinging pendulum. Is it swinging over yes or no? If you've done it properly, you'll get a yes. Now ask a baseline question, it should be something that can be answered with a chart and something you can verify. Maybe something you don't know, but could look up. I don't recommend yes/no questions as a baseline if you can help it. Or questions you already know the answer to, because then you may doubt yourself and/or the validity of the spirit if it answers correctly.

You can repeat this exercise as often as you wish.

TIPS

1. Stay relaxed and keep your mind quiet.
2. Keep your hand steady.
3. If you get wrong answers consistently, consider that you may be the one hindering the contact with a spirit. This can be due to disbelief, fear of communicating with spirits, or even a playful spirit you don't have a good enough working relationship with.
4. Start by communicating with Daemons you work with often. By doing this you are more likely to

get good results while simultaneously learning how to "feel" Daemonic energy, thus teaching yourself the difference between a Daemon and your higher self or intuition.

Scrying

Scrying (also skrying) is a form of divination in which you peer into a reflective surface and visually see images. Sometimes these images appear in your minds-eye, and sometimes they appear as real ocular images. This method of divination will work best for people who have some clairvoyant abilities. The three most common forms of scrying are mirror, crystal, and bowl (water) scrying. Less discussed are fire/smoke scrying and blood scrying. I'll discuss both of these later in this chapter.

First, I think it's prudent for seers and mediums to know and understand that scrying is a big part of the old ceremonial magickal texts. Enochian and Goetia are both rife with Scrying. I contend that Goetia is, in fact, a scrying rite. The magician is seeking to evoke the Daemonic into the triangle of art, into a black mirror. I know a lot of ceremonialists who disagree here, thinking it's dangerous to evoke a Daemon into one's own reflection. Perhaps it is if you're terrified of Daemons and spirit communication. These people will insist that within the triangle of art is NOT a scrying mirror, but rather a portal from which the Daemon can arise from the floor. I mention this because learning the art of scrying and honing your skills can significantly enhance and boost your goetic work. This is also why many old manuscripts talk about having an "operator" and another participant, the "medium", during this kind of work.

Now let's talk a little about prep-work. To prepare your scrying equipment you can anoint the devices directly with oleums of Daemons for divination, a divination oil (see preparation of the seer/medium for a recipe) or you can add appropriate sigils to the devices themselves. For scrying mirrors, you can put the sigils on the frame or the back of the mirror directly. For crystals, you should probably leave them intact and untouched because you want their surfaces to be clean and free of fingerprints or smudge. You can set them in salt, wash them, and run them through incense smoke to regularly clean and clear them. For bowls, you can paint sigils directly onto the outside of the bowls. As with most divination sessions if you're just starting out you probably ought to consider working within a balanced, Daemonically charged circle for both balance and to keep unwanted influences (entities or energies) out of the way while you work. Obviously the more experienced the person, the less of a need for balance since you'll clearly know how to balance yourself if anything goes amiss.

Creating the Mirror:

You can buy a scrying mirror. They're basically mirrors with a black backing. Others are highly polished black stones or pieces of black glass. Or, if you have some time and ambition, you can create your own mirror. Making a scrying mirror is a relatively simple process.

The first step is to buy a picture frame with glass intact (or a piece of glass that will fit into a frame). Do not buy plastic! Make sure it's real glass and the thicker the glass, the better because it gives more depth. Choose a frame that has some aesthetic appeal for you (i.e. something you really like). You can get frames at dollar stores and thrift stores inexpensively.

Remove the glass from the frame and clean it completely (same process for a mirror). With some glossy black oil based enamel paint, paint one side of the glass (or the back silver side of the mirror). You will need to apply as many coats as necessary to make sure no light passes through. Allow the paint to dry completely between coats.

Paint any sigils or symbols you wish on your frame. Finally, put the glass (or mirror) back into the frame, the paint side of the glass on the inside. Make sure you have some cardboard or felt board against the painted side to keep the glass from getting scuffed. Use a collector plate stand to prop your Scrying mirror up (or if you're using a frame that came with a stand, that can work too) and you're done. You can get collector plate stands at hobby and craft stores and usually large discount stores like Wal-Mart or Target.

Finally – you can use a regular mirror. However, many people won't get results with a regular mirror unless they're very sensitive. You can try it and if it works for you, great. But if it doesn't work, try a black mirror.

One of the important things I didn't mention in DGDM is my complete dislike of silver mirrors for scrying. My personal preference is for black mirrors because the images aren't as clear. I prefer my images a little murky, but only because seeing too clearly in the mirror can be a horrifying experience for those of us who are extremely sensitive. Not to mention for those of us who are very sensitive, there are some Daemons who will use that sensitivity to force you to fear face (it's what they do). Not out of malevolence, mind you, but rather for your own good. Quite frankly I'm not keen on looking directly into the eyes of things that look like they've escaped from a recent blockbuster horror film. Call me a wuss, but I contend that most folks would agree with me. It's great to pretend we're all brave and badass, but when you actually see that shit – it affects you, and not always in positive ways. Ask anyone who has worked with violent death day in and day out for years. It's not sick, or cool, or badass, or metal. It's emotionally traumatizing. So – fair warning – if you are a strong medium, I'd use silver mirrors with caution. Black mirrors will give you excellent results and not give feisty Daemons the opportunity to really mess with you.

A Mirror Exercise:

Sit in a dark room in front of the prepared scrying mirror. Flank the mirror with two candles. Completely relax your body. Make sure you are comfortable. Open your eyes and look into the mirror. See your own reflection. Watch your own reflection fade. As your reflection fades your initial response is likely to bring it back into focus. But practice getting past that initial urge to focus, because it's after your reflection fades into the darkness that the shapes and images will begin to come. This is a great practice for those who can get to the "fade" part of the operation, but can go no further. You basically need to practice going into the "fade", beyond it, and within it to draw out the images you seek.

Crystals:

There are numerous crystals you can use for gazing. Some are cut in the shape of pyramids or other geometrics. The most popular are crystal gazing balls. Glass can be used in place of crystal, but some believe that vibration of the crystal itself allegedly lends better to gazing/Scrying. Regardless, the ball should be kept clean and free of fingerprints and dust. I prefer clear quartz, but I know people who prefer Rose Quartz and even Smokey Quartz. I've actually had the rare experience of actually catching images of spirits in the crystal with a camera. To prepare the crystal, wash it in salt water, wave it through frankincense or sage smoke, dry it with a soft cloth, then draw the invocation seal (see Complete Book of Demonolatry) in the air over it with your fingers while invoking the Daemonic force you wish to be present.

Perhaps one of the most interesting rituals I was ever given, from the Daemonic, for scrying with crystal is this:

"Upon the plate you place beneath a shroud of black cloth. Call upon the Daemons of old to bring forth their wisdom. Sprinkle rain water around the crystal. Chant their Enns and gaze, with eyes part closed, into the depths of the abyss. There, betwixt the rays of candlelight, one who agrees to give counsel shall come forth. Speak with him then and he shall give truthful answers if it serves you best."

Scrying Bowls:

Your average Scrying bowl is dark in color (either black or some other dark color) and you put water, ink, oil, specially formulated "milks" or blood into the bowl for Scrying to create the reflective surface. If you're not reading shapes and are simply looking for a reflective surface, the scrying fluids used in the bowl should be of even color. So mix liquids beforehand, for example if you're diluting blood in water, or ink in water, or using blood or ink in oil. Some liquids separate. In some methods of Scrying this is desirable. In others, it's not. Depending on whether you're reading the shapes in the water (as with tea leaf reading) then you might use oil in a water-based fluid, or vice versa. If you're not doing that kind of "reading" or Scrying – a fluid, solid color with no separation is best. Inks, blood, and waters often work well together. Oil is one of those substances that you can use alone, or with a different type of water. Yes – there are different types of prepared waters and milks used for scrying! More about that in a second.

In some instances a lighter bowl may be preferred, especially if one is reading shapes from the blood or ink. This preference is going to vary from sorcerer to sorcerer. All of our gifts work differently from our fellow magi, so feel free to experiment and find out what works best for you.

Some Daemonolaters I know have even painted seals into the bottom of their bowls. I, personally, find that rather distracting to the reflective surface or the formation of shapes.

Scrying Waters

Scrying waters were actually quite common once-upon-a-time. These days, however, the practice seems to have fallen out of fashion. The following are recipes for scrying waters given to me by the Daemons I've worked with over the years. My favorite is Leviathan's "Foresight Blend" with the heavy clary sage overtones. For rather obvious reasons (for me anyway) it enhances my sight a great deal. Please do NOT INGEST any of the scrying waters here. Many of them contain poisonous substances. Use caution when working with these plants as well. You can also mix these blends with olive oil to creating scrying oil blends! Oils are usually gently heated first before being cooled and bottled. So without further ado...

Leviathan's "Foresight Blend"

- Two cups of rain water (or distilled water)
- Five drops of clary sage oil
- One pinch of mandrake root (or five drops of mandrake tincture)
- One pinch of fine ground belladonna leaves (or five drops of belladonna tincture.)

You can adjust the amount of clary sage to your liking for scent. Mix the tinctures (or plant matter) and oils in the water and let them steep in a dark jar (or a regular clear jar in a root cellar or cool, dry place) for a full moon cycle. If you used plant material, strain the liquid and use. If you used already strained tinctures and the oil, you can use it directly without straining. About ½ cup is used for each divination session. Distilling your own water is one method to give this water (and all waters for that matter) a "power-up".

Water of Ashtaroth/Astaroth

In two cups of rain water, steep nine yellow rose petals (dried is fine), one bay leaf, a whole dandelion root, one hibiscus flower (dried is fine). Stir the mixture with a willow branch then let steep for one week before use. Strain and use. Use this water to divine about relationships and love.

Water of Lucifuge

With two cups of rain water (or distilled water) create a wormwood hydrosol. Add to this three dried yarrow flowers. Let this steep for at least a week (a month is better). Strain and then use. About ½ cup per divination session.

Eurynomous' Water of the Dead

Two teaspoons of dried wormwood leaves, one inch of mandrake root, one teaspoon belladonna and some willow bark and, during the dark moon, mix it in a jar with two cups of distilled water and a teaspoon of black ink. Bury the water in the earth for a full month. Unearth it, strain it, and use. This water is used ½ cup at a time, and should be used for divination sessions where you are seeking to contact the dead or the Daemons of death.

A Scrying Milk Recipe

To 1/4 cup tincture of benzoin made with vodka add one tablespoon powdered storax, one pinch of powdered cinnamon and one pinch of powdered nutmeg. Let steep for one month from full moon to full moon, then strain, bottle in amber bottles, and use. Light colored scrying bowls are best.

Lecanomancy

This is a method by which one drops objects into scrying waters and then reads. Stones, herbs, milks, inks, blood, etc… can be dropped into the water. Usually shapes are read or the disturbance in the water is read.

The Methods of Scrying with Blood and Oil

Let's talk more about the liquids used in scrying and the methods. The liquids are not always put in bowls. Let me say that up front because it's a common misconception that all liquid substance scrying is done in a bowl.

One particular method of blood scrying says to: *Prick the left ring finger six to nine times, squeeze the finger to release the blood, then swirl it around in the water counter-clockwise. The water will change to a pinkish hue and if you look within, you will see your fate.* To divine for someone else using this method, you would use their blood and the same method.

To divine by shapes that appear in the water, you would allow the blood to run from your finger into the bowl, not stirring the water, thus allowing the blood to form shapes at its will. To divine for someone else, use the same method. The beauty of this particular method is that for women, if you collect a vial of menstrual blood, you can pour it into the bowl and save yourself a sore finger.

Some also say which finger the blood is taken from has significance. The thumb is for work. The forefinger is for creativity. The middle finger is health. The ring finger is for love and friendships. Finally, the pinky is for spiritual matters.

Some people who practice blood scrying with their own blood will sometimes hire a phlebotomist to collect vials of blood that they keep in their refrigerator until it's needed. Some people find use of their own blood sacrilegious (non-traditional Daemonolaters usually) and will only kill animals. I personally do not condone animal sacrifice unless the ritual is of the utmost importance, the animal is killed humanely and with respect, and the flesh of the animal is used for your nourishment afterward. I find animal sacrifice that isn't respectful an act of cowardice. By sacrificing an animal with cruelty or disregard for life – a magus sacrifices nothing of himself and is unworthy. Not everyone agrees with me on this point and that's his/her choice. Please take care to observe local laws.

With magickal inks, the preparation is much the same. Either the ink can be swirled through the water, or simply dropped in with a dropper or poured from a vial. It depends if you're simply coloring the water to enhance your vision, or reading the shapes within the water.

If you are scrying with oil there are a lot of methods out there. Research led me to the Greek Magical Papyri where, I was assured by about fifty of the same copied and pasted internet articles and some popular occult authors that, I would find detailed examples of these methods. However, none of them could tell me what those methods were. So I'm going to tell you to save you the aggravating task of having to read the entire Papyri for yourself or chase your tail on an internet web search proving that no one actually writes their own shit anymore (or reads the Greek Magical Papyri despite their reference to it). I do recommend you read the papyri if you have the time and interest to do so.

In one instance, olive oil (always olive oil from that part of the world) was put on the thumb nail of the person being read for. There, the seer would gaze into the nail and read that person's destiny. Other times olive oil, in which had been steeped divining herbs, was poured into a bowl and the seer would read from that. Pools of water and perfumed oils meant to enhance the seer's vision were also used. (See water recipes above and note that they can also be used with olive oil.)

Tea Leaf Reading

It would be odd for me to write an entire book about Daemonic divination, or divination alone, without discussing tea leaf reading. The premise of tea leaf reading is much the same as "shape" reading. First, you make tea for someone using loose tea leaves. You allow the tea to steep and the tea leaves to settle at the bottom. The person you're reading for drinks the tea until just a little liquid, maybe a tablespoon, remains in the cup along with the leaves. The seer then takes the cup from the person and reads the shapes the leaves make and the images from the reflections in the water. *To add a Daemonic Divination twist to this, make a tea of chamomile and hibiscus and steep it in a cup painted (on the outside) with Daemonic sigils and anointed with a divination oil on the bottom. Either you drink the tea (if you're reading for yourself) or have the person you're reading for drink the tea, then read the leaves and images as usual.*

You can employ this method before larger divination sessions to also enhance your divination abilities as well, since this tea blend will enhance your vision. Almost like a precursor to give you additional insight into the divination you are about to perform, or to discover if you should work with a particular client. The uses for this method are only limited by one's own mind.

Fire (and Smoke) Scrying

In fire scrying, one peers into the flames to see visions. There are also methods of divination that use peering into smoke from a smoldering fire (or incense) that you can also consider. It is believed that in smoke a seer can see shapes or visions just as with fire. In Daemonic fire scrying, the Daemons are invoked before the session. Whether or not you create a balanced ritual space is up to you. I do recommend creating that balanced ritual space for beginners just for the sake of balance and keeping the Daemonic energy high, thus the likelihood of attracting nothing but Daemonic spirits, but if you know yourself well enough, have worked with Daemons a great deal and feel confident enough, you can skip that step. Next, incense is thrown into the fire. If you are divining with smoke, the incense is thrown onto the smoldering coal(s) or wood. You can, theoretically use any incense dedicated to a specific Daemon, or blends exclusively created for fire and smoke scrying, like the following:

Fire Scrying Incense:

- 10 Dried Juniper Berries (or two tablespoons dried Juniper)

- 1/2 cup dried cedar wood
- 1/4 cup dried sandalwood

If you are using a charcoal and burning indoors to simply enhance a different divination method, make sure all ingredients are powdered. If you are scrying in a fire pit, go ahead and leave bigger chunks of the dried woody bits because it will burn slower.

This incense is meant to be used in a fire pit for actual fire scrying. The seer should invoke any Daemons desired, then throw about a tablespoon of incense into the fire, scry, and repeat.

Basic Scrying Incense

For all methods and operations of divination. Burn in well ventilated areas due to the awful smell.

- 1/2 cup of mugwort
- 1/4 cup of wormwood

Again, if using on a charcoal, make sure the herbs are finely ground. If using during fire scrying in a fire pit, you can leave the herbs coarse.

A Fire Scrying Exercise

Effective scrying requires excellent meditation skills. This exercise is a fire meditation that you can do in front of a bonfire, fire pit, gas fireplace in your home, or even a simple candle flame.

Make sure you are comfortable and relaxed. Stare into the flames and relax your mind. Listen. Lose yourself in the flame. Become the flame. Feel its warmth. Bask in its glow. Whisper the Daemonic enn of the Daemon you wish to invoke. If images begin to appear, just let them come. Don't try to see them harder if they are unclear, simply let them come and go. Stay relaxed. Watch. Listen. At ten minutes stop. Repeat this exercise as needed.

How to Scry

Within a prepared ritual space, flank your Scrying device with candles, then gaze into your Scrying device and clear your mind. Completely let go and allow the images to come. Usually the reflective surface will fade to black (or seem hazy or smoky) and then the images will come forth. Sometimes they're clear, sometimes not. Try your best not to give a voice to the images, let them come and go. Just remember them. If you try too hard to see, you may inadvertently stifle the flow of imagery. When you pause, write down what you've seen or say aloud what you see (having a recorder there, human or electronic is handy), giving your mind time to process the images. If we try too soon to process and define the images, we can end up stilting the flow of the images and holding ourselves back from stronger images.

For some people, scrying is not easy because the images are far too disturbing or unsettling for them to handle. Others won't get images at all because they have no gifts for clairvoyance. Some people with clairsentience or clairaudience claim they can hear or know from a scrying device and the mirror simply helps them hear or know better. Some people will actually use a mirror to channel. The only way to know if Scrying works for you is to try it. If it doesn't, there are plenty of other divination devices and methods to try and learn. If the images are weak – you can continue to practice and hone your skill as eventually they'll become stronger.

For some, when scrying with ink, milk, herbs or blood, or in smoke or flame, the seer will see shapes, like wolves or triangles. These shapes will have meaning to the seer and the seer can interpret them as one might interpret dream images, for example. Generally if I see anything to do with cats during dream work or divinatory work, I know that it has something to do with publishing. It's one hundred percent accurate all of the time. That's my personal interpretation of cat imagery. You will have to figure out your own symbol interpretation and that could take years. I know, most of us would love a symbol dictionary to refer to, but the reality is that not all things mean the same things to all people. You can start by using dream dictionaries to help you interpret symbolism from your scrying sessions – as seeing ability relies on the same subconscious part of the brain to be activated during waking states. However, after years of practice you will most likely find that certain images mean different things to you than what's written in your standard dream dictionary. Go with your gut on this. In divination – the first response is usually the correct one.

The best advice I can give aspiring seers is to learn to let your mind go. One of our biggest obstacles in divination, as physical beings, is getting past not only the sensations of our physical bodies, but letting go of our physical realities and what we deem possible vs. impossible. Learning to let go of physical reality can make a huge difference in the success of your divinatory operations. The only way you can learn to do this is to practice letting go and allowing your emotions and natural responses reign supreme no matter how irrational or bizarre they seem to the logical mind (just like the dream state).

More Scrying Exercises:

Exercise I.

This is a "getting-to-know-you" exercise with your scrying device. It can work with fire and smoke as well. But for a Fire specific exercise, see the Fire Scrying Section. Sit down with your scrying device in front of you. The goal of this session isn't to try to divine anything or see anything or even to communicate. It's a quiet meditation with the scrying device. Take your scrying device into your prepared ritual space, or someplace comfortable and quiet. You can do this by candlelight or even soft lamp light or dim indirect daylight. Close your eyes. Take a few deep, measured breaths. Quiet your mind. Listen. Open your eyes and look at your device. If a mirror, let your eyes travel over every square inch. If a crystal or bowl, look it over. Examine it. Note all of its curves or edges or lines. Examine the reflective surface. Touch it and feel the energy of it. (This latter bit works better with closed eyes.) Then, if you can gaze into that reflective surface, do so. Delve into it and examine how it reacts to the light in the room. Now if you find yourself seeing shapes or images in the scrying surface, don't panic or stop yourself, just let it happen. Your goal in this exercise is to simply observe.

Exercise II.

This is a "connecting" exercise that can also be useful in other forms of divination as well as scrying. Again, in a quiet and comfortable spot with your scrying device in front of you (flanked by candles of course), focus on the Daemon you wish to contact. Whisper, chant, or intone the enn to call the Daemon to you. Keep your eyes closed at first, making you more aware of the changing energy currents around you. Feel the Daemonic energy enter the room or ritual space. Feel it come toward you, surround you, and infuse your device with its essence. Now open your eyes and see it. See your divination device glowing with Daemonic energy. Feel the pulsating energy with your hands. Take a few deep, measured breaths and then use your device. Once you make it past the initial stage of reflection "fade", just let the images, thoughts and feelings come, letting go of all need to control it. Repeat this exercise often for maximum results. Yes, basically this is scrying practice, if you will.

Reading Daemonic Sigils

Contrary to popular belief, the idea of Reading Daemonic Sigils drawn on cards, carved into or painted onto stones or clay is not anything new. Reading Daemonic Sigils is a fairly old practice; probably as old as the practice of working with Rune Stones and Tarot Cards. The concept is pretty much the same.

Each card, stone, piece of wood, or clay stone has painted or engraved on it a sigil of a Daemonic name. Traditionally, a person makes his or her own cards, clay tablets, wooden seals, or stones using sigils of Daemons (s)he is familiar with. These are kept in a bag or jar and when a situation arises that the person needs guidance on, one of the cards, stones or clay pieces is pulled.

Whichever Daemonic sigil you pull is the answer to the inquiry (or the wisdom you seek in the situation). So, for example, if you are angry with a co-worker and you need to know which action to take and you pull Unsere, this would mean you should try to be understanding and work through your differences with the co-worker because things could get better. If you pull Amducius, a confrontation might be prudent or imminent. If you pull Belphagore, it could mean it's time to update your resume` and you should seek employment elsewhere.

You can also use standard Tarot Card layouts (you can find some in the next chapter) in much the same way by pulling a sigil for each position and then reading the sigil (by understanding what each Daemon represents) based on the position in which it falls. See the Tarot Card section to learn more about positioning and performing readings in a prescribed sequence.

I would go into further detail on this method in this book except that I've already written and entire book on divination by way of Daemonic sigils called *Sigillum Diaboli* that covers the topic pretty extensively. So please see that book for an in depth look at using Daemonic sigils for divination.

As a side note, a reader recently told me he had plans to make a set of divination bones with Daemonic sigils on them. So if you practice bone divination that might be something for you to explore.

Tarot Cards

Tarot Cards are one of the most common forms of divination. Now while you're usually not contacting the Daemonic through the cards (or you could be), you can still use cards within a balanced ritual space in order to connect with your own internal Daemonic wisdom or insight. Usually – reading cards is about connecting with your higher self and your intuition in order to find the answers. By reading the cards the intuitive can get a sense of what has happened, what the present situation is, and what will happen if the current path is followed. This means that the outcome presented by the cards is not fixed.

To read the cards, the person doing the reading may have the person the reading is for shuffle the cards then cut the cards three times toward him/herself (if the question is about them personally) or cut them three times away from themselves if the question is about another person. If the person the reading is for is not present, the reader can concentrate on that person and perform the reading that way. Very sensitive readers can give very functional and accurate readings from long distances. To begin the reading, the reader will lay the cards out and read the cards starting from the past, moving to the present, and finally to the final outcome.

Some readers will read the inverse meaning of cards, others will not. From my experience the *good* readers will not merely memorize the little booklet that came with their set of tarot cards and give everyone a stock reading of what the cards allegedly mean. Instead, true empaths, intuitives, and mediums will have studied the cards a great deal, will read from the symbolism of the card and what the cards mean to them and will use the cards as a tool to sort out their empathic or intuitive feelings about a situation.

A very common tarot layout is called the Celtic Cross.

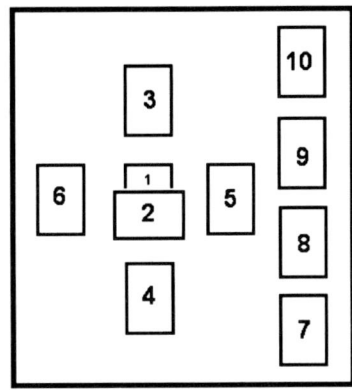

1. Present Position

2. What crosses your present position.
3. What is influencing the present position (what's in the asker's head).
4. Distant past foundation.
5. What lies ahead.
6. Recent past foundation.
7. The path to the final outcome.
8. The path to the final outcome. Influences.
9. The path to the final outcome. More Influences.
10. The final outcome.

Additional cards can be laid out on each of these areas to gain more insight into a specific influence or situation.

Or, a more simple layout is the past, present, future layout where only three cards are pulled. There are numerous methods by which to read. Even Daemonic Sigils (and even Rune Stones) can be pulled out and read using much the same layouts.

To learn to read the cards you will need to practice for many years before you get good at it. Each card is part of a sentence. If you pull more than one card for each position (I do) you will read each card in context with the one next to it. For different people and different readings – the same card could mean something different depending on where it is in the *sentence*. The Chariot and the Sun next to the Ace of Coins might suggest a financial windfall prosperous to the person the reading is for. The Chariot and The Sun next to the Ace of Cups could mean a wedding or the beginnings of a beautiful friendship. The Devil next to The Tower next to the Three of Coins could mean financial troubles that are enough to cause a change in how someone lives his/her life. The Devil next to the Three of Coins next to the Knight of Swords could mean financial problems due to a child, friend or sibling who is irresponsible. So while the basic meanings may be ever-present, none of your "sentences" will be the same.

It's okay to start learning to read by using the books that give you a general idea of what each card means. The person serious about learning to read cards, however, must eventually graduate past the pull the card, regurgitate memorized information, repeat - stage. This involves taking time to meditate on each card and write down everything that card means to you. **A valuable exercise** is to get one of those color-your-own tarot decks and basically to meditate on each card and color your own, adding your own symbolism.

Once you've attached a meaning to a card they will become easier to read. Cards can also be a valuable meditation device to use during ritual and magickal workings as representations of what you want to accomplish with the working. Anyone who cannot graduate past the "use the book" or who thinks they have to memorize the cards in order to read them is one who likely doesn't have a gift for accessing the internal intuition required to read cards. If you find you cannot, after years of practice, read the cards without use of a book, or if you have had to memorize the book and cannot go beyond it, consider this may not be a good divination device for you.

Remember that all methods of divination are just tools you can use to tap something you already have. They make reading a situation or person easier through more tangible means (i.e. images, sentences, a physically swinging pendulum or moving planchette, etc…).

I recommending consecrating and dedicating at least one tarot deck to your Daemonic divination work.

See the ritual toward the end of this book for more information.

Tarot Exercises:

1. Spend several months doing meditations on each card. It doesn't have to be long. Keep a tarot notebook. Look at each card, examine it. Understand what it means by the book, then write down what it means to you. This meditation need only take 10-15 minutes per day. Do this for each card until you've gone through all 72.
2. Once you've completed the above exercise, get a color-your-own deck and add symbolism you find relevant to each card. Feel free to use other decks for inspiration.

TIPS:

- Some believe that you should never buy your first tarot deck for yourself. Instead, it should be a gift.
- Keep your dedicated deck (for the first few years of use at least) wrapped in purple or gold cloth. You can use black if you prefer. Eventually it will become so saturated with Daemonic essence that it won't matter.
- When you find a deck you really "click" with, buy an extra set to have on hand just in case something happens to the first one.
- Take your time choosing a deck. Find a store that will let you take your time and look at decks. Our local pagan store actually has binders full of decks with comfortable chairs so people can sit down and go through the books to find a deck that speaks to them. Don't just buy a random deck. A bad deck that isn't your cup of tea could hinder your ability to

learn to read the cards. I always recommend people start with decks that have clear, clean, solid imagery. If it's too obscure or scant – learning to read from such cards can be a virtual impossibility and memorize, regurgitate, repeat will be your only option.

Channeling

This entire chapter remains mostly the same from *The Daemonolater's Guide to Daemonic Magick*, except that I discuss possession vs. channeling and automatic writing methods here

Channeling is basically a process wherein you allow a Daemonic presence (or any spiritual presence for that matter) to take over your body so that it can perform physical action, or more often, can use your mouth to speak directly to others in the room. Some people call it possession, but let's be frank for a moment. Possession suggests being taken over against one's will. If you are willfully allowing a spirit to take over your body and you are still in control to some degree, that's not possession – that's channeling and that's what we're discussing here.

The only truly possessed individuals I've run across are writers, artists, and musicians, even scientists or other creative types who are *possessed* by an idea from the Daimonic/Daemonic muse (whether internal or external). Real possession has real purpose behind it. Daemons don't just take over people to make them cuss, masturbate, convulse, spit, throw up, or insult members of the clergy. It's my opinion that that's a ridiculous Christian fear with no basis in reality. I believe that most Christian possession cases are just repressed or mentally disturbed individuals seeking attention.

Oftentimes, I don't recommend channeling unless you are working with several people. Not so much because it's dangerous (if you know what you're doing or do it within a prepared and balanced ritual space!) or anything like that, but rather there's not often as much use for channeling unless you're with other people. Sometimes, the person channeling can get lost in the feeling of having their mind disconnected from their body, and won't remember what was said. Other times, the person channeling could panic (if it's their first time) and it's useful to have someone else there to help bring them back from the experience.

In this section I'll explain some merging techniques and controlled channeling techniques that will help you channel. If during the exercises you do go into channeling, don't panic. The Daemon will recognize when you're ready to return and will leave your body. I've only heard of two people who have actually passed out from the experience. This is why you'll want to perform this operation on the ground (with a blanket nearby just in case) or where you won't have any danger of falling and hurting yourself (i.e. like sitting in a chair).

If you are a part of a group or have an open-minded friend, you can do your experiments with these people. The method is that once you invoke and merge with the Daemon, the group asks questions and the Daemon answers.

Why Channel?

Channeling can be useful during group divination. I have a friend who used to do weekly group channeling lessons wherein the Daemon they were working with, Belial (hence in-part the reasoning in the title of this book, praise Paimon), put the group through guided meditations and offered practical advice on self-work. Unfortunately I was unable to attend their meetings so did not witness this first hand. But from those in the group I talked to, they were getting a lot from it.

I've personally used channeling (with a Daemonic entity) in paranormal investigations as a way to identify what is happening in a house or location.

How does one channel?

There are three basic steps to channeling. Invocation, merging, and allowing the Daemon to take over the body. The last part is the hardest for most people because it's instinctive for us to want to maintain control of our bodies. For others, this is going to come quite naturally.

A Note of Warning:

When I say channeling is not dangerous, I mean, it's not dangerous for mentally stable individuals who are working within a well prepared and balanced ritual space. This means you have invoked Daemonic entities into the space so that nothing else can get to you or disturb the work or slip into your body while you're open to it. Not all spirits or entities are Daemonic and not all are friendly. I suggest working with the Daemons Ashtaroth and Azlyn (aka Azyn) during divination using a pentagram ritual configuration at which each point an elemental is invoked (don't forget your fifth element) using the appropriate Enns. Ashtaroth and Azlyn would be invoked from the center.

A Channeling Exercise:

Meditate on the Daemon of your choice. Use an Enn to invoke the Daemon if you wish. Allow their energy to surround you. Surrender to it. Merge with it. Remember your breath. Relax. Allow all emotions, feelings, and thoughts to flow freely. Their thoughts become your thoughts and vice versa. You are intertwined with this Daemon.

[Note - the point of this exercise is not to BECOME the Daemon. That is impossible. However, you can merge with a Daemon by intertwining energies empathically.]

To Channel, you simply let go and allow the Daemon to take over when you feel that you and the Daemon's energies are merged sufficiently.

If you are doing automatic writing with this, simply add pen and paper to the mix. Let go and allow the Daemonic force control of your hands.

Remember that if you want to be returned to control of your consciousness, just ask. Most Daemons won't stay unless they have good reason or an important message.

Leviathan had this to say: *Confinement to the physical body is prison. It is too small and cannot hold nor sustain* *us for long before faltering and withering under the weight of our fervor.*

What to Expect:

Many people describe the feeling of hearing someone talking with their voice, but it not being them. They often report feeling disconnected from their own mind and body and surrounded in blackness. I have had this same experience. The second you feel panicked or like you want to return into your mind to regain control, the Daemon will usually step aside and allow you back in. I say usually because I have heard of rare instances where a Daemon stayed for several hours past its welcome because it had a very important message to impart. I've never heard of an instance of this continuing for more than several hours though.

More importantly you should know the people involved could get really freaked out by a Daemon or spirit being channeled. It's important you discuss with the participants what they should expect so that no one is caught off guard or panics during a session. The others present should expect the medium's voice and personality to completely change. (S)he might use words or phrases (s)he would never use, her face may contort and take on a different appearance, her voice may sound gruff or even plural, and in some instances those present may experience paranormal phenomena during the session including actually seeing physically manifested entities separate or merge with the host medium, stray lights and shadows, sounds, and even objects moving. I have experienced all of these phenomena at least once during a channeling session, so expect it just in case.

To leave the state of Channeling at will, simply tell the Daemon (obviously in your mind) that you would like to return to your body now. You should find yourself back in your body and in full control of your faculties. You may also feel like you're waking up from a nap. Channeling can be a very strong and unbalancing experience. If you find yourself imbalanced by channeling (as being connected to a Daemon like that is like being plugged into a power plant), be sure to balance yourself before and after each session.

Automatic Writing

With channeling comes a divination form many of you reading are familiar with – automatic writing. A lot of famous mediums have used automatic writing as a method of spirit communication. I have used automatic writing to glean Daemonic wisdom for this book and I regularly use it as a method for divination when doing readings for clients.

Automatic writing works on the premise of connecting to, and channeling the spirit, Daemonic force, or even the higher self, focusing on questions, and having the spirit you are connecting with answer via the written word. Sure, you could do the same thing with a spirit board, but allowing the spirit to take over your body and write it out is a far more efficient method, especially if you have no one else there to record the session. It's the next best thing to allowing the spirit to speak directly to others through you.

To do automatic writing you need three things. The medium, a good pen (or pencil, though if it breaks you're screwed), and a pad of paper. In this instance the medium would simply relax, open him/herself up to the spirit they seek to contact, hold the pen and paper, and allow the spirit to come through and write what it has to say. For those of you who aren't luddites and don't mind a more non-traditional approach, try opening a blank document in your word processing program and channeling in front of your computer keyboard. You can get just as effective results. I have anyway.

One of the ways I explain the difference in connections in divination, channeling and ascension is this: Divination is like sitting with someone at a table in a familiar setting. You're in each other's space. You won't feel alone. If you're in your home, you may get that same sensation you get when you have guests over. Ascension, on the other hand, is like visiting someone else's house that you're not familiar with. You're not alone and you're in unfamiliar surroundings. It may not be comfortable, and the host(s) can be unpredictable. Finally, Channeling is rather intimate – even more than lovemaking. In channeling you are willingly sharing the most hidden parts of yourself, your psyche and your body, with another consciousness.

As always – feel free to experiment with teas, scents, and tinctures to enhance your channeling and divination experiences.

TIPS:
- Teas and tinctures work great for channeling and ascension. If you're having issues getting over that last hurdle, give them a try, but use them sparingly and responsibly. Make sure they don't become a crutch.
- The key to most good divination sessions are a calm, quiet mind, and a willingness to listen.

Ascension

This particular section about ascension remains the same as it was in *Daemonolater's Guide*. While some minor changes may have been made to the text, I didn't add much only because I felt this section was rather complete in its original form.

Ascension is a method by which we can commune with the Daemonic Divine on an alternate plane of consciousness. Think of it as connecting with the universal consciousness. It's the best of both Insight Meditation and Channeling, but it all happens in the ascended meditative state. Most people receive images during ascension, making it a very effective meditative state for learning more about the Daemons and their plane of existence.

Many Daemonolaters use ascension for divination, to learn how to perform certain rites, to see physical manifestations of the Daemons, and to learn more about the nature of the Daemonic. Ascension is also an effective tool for self-work, meaning the Daemons will often impart wisdom through the practitioner's ascended states.

To begin, most people will use what I call a "Ready Ascension Formula", meaning a ritual to ascend to that particular plane of consciousness wherein we meet the

Daemonic Divine head on. As you gain more experience and confidence, you'll discover you have developed your own method to ascend to this particular state. The following exercises will teach beginning ascension practitioners helpful methods to learn to ascend, and will help seasoned practitioners hone their skills and analyze their own methods of ascension.

Ready Ascension Formulas:

Many Daemonolaters believe that ascension is best achieved when we face our fears because it brings our awareness into ourselves and makes us more sensitive to the ascended state. That's often why those who don't practice "fear facing" will report their ascension attempts always result in cloudy, faded, or dark images that won't clear up.

PLEASE NOTE: *You can substitute Tiger Balm (you can buy this from any drug store in the section where they sell sports creams) for anointing oil and replace incense recipes with an incense of your choice. You also don't necessarily need incenses or oils. Those with allergies may choose not to use incense at all. The primary purpose in these formulas is to stimulate the senses to invoke atmosphere and a heightened state of awareness. Their secondary purpose is to invoke the proper conditions for effective ascension. But you can reach an ascended state without them.*

To Ascend to the Daemonic Plane
Richard Dukanté

1 part rose
2 parts chamomile
1 part camphor

Mix into oil and anoint temples. Place a parchment on which are drawn 12 Daemonic sigils of your discretion. Place this beneath your mattress or beneath your sleeping place. Light a white candle. Place an image of yourself outside yourself and project your consciousness into it. Go through black caverns and face your fears one by one. Only then shall you emerge onto the plane. If you do not, your fears have not been faced.

Invocation To Speak With a Daemon
(from Dukanté grimoire)

The Daemon Conjuration Of Richard Dukanté (circa 1963 - the Grimoire of Richard Dukante Book 1 Page 50) Being a working wherein the Daemon of the practitioner's choice may be called upon willfully.

Upon the altar must stand three tapers. One of Black, One of White, One of the castor's element. Within the Castor's taper the Daemon's name must be inscribed upon it along with the name of Satan. [meaning actual - SATAN]

Present also must be the dagger and chalice of water taken from a flowing river or from the falling rain.

The invocation incense shall be burned within the thurible during the entire rite: 2 Parts Sandalwood, 5 Parts Graveyard Dust [mullein], and 3 Parts Devil's Claw.

You shall begin by lighting the tapers upon the altar after having writ the aforementioned inscriptions on the center taper. Set the incense alight within the thurible. Cast the circle by invoking each element in the language of Daemons –

- Earth - Belial - *Lirach Tasa Vefa Wehlc Belial*
- Air - Lucifer - *Renich Tasa Uberaca Biasa Icar Lucifer*
- Fire - Flereous - *Ganic Tasa Fubin Flereous*
- Water - Leviathan- *Jedan Tasa Hoet Naca Leviathan*

Begin the Invocation: I, [your name], do invite thee, [Daemon's name]. In the name of Satan [or insert the name of your highest deity], I request you come forth.

Hence you shall draw your own blood from your palm and let three drops fall into the chalice. Mingle it with the water and invite all present to drink from it. Do not drink from your own blood lest you invite the Daemon into you.

You shall draw a circle upon the ground the width of the taper at least. Within this circle, inscribe the sigil of the Daemon you doth conjure. If this sigil is unavailable, use an inverse pentagram or DZ. You shall pour the remainder of the chalice contents within the circle - for it is your energy the Daemon will use to rise. "'Tis this energy that is blood."

Over the circle you must say:

Reayha bacana lyan remé quim [name of Daemon].

Place the castor's candle within the circle. From this circle - the Daemon shall emerge from the flame and you may speak with him freely until the candle is extinguished.

Finding Your Personal Key

A "key" is basically your own method of entering the Daemonic plane. For some, it's an actual key used to unlock a specific door to the Daemonic plane. For others, the key is a sigil, place, or thing they visualize that will help them get onto the Daemonic Plane. For me, the sigil of Delepitore, merely thinking of it, will often pull me directly into an ascended state. I've trained my mind to do this through repeating the visualization each time I practice a session of ascension. This alleviates the long process of ascending (through visualizing halls and doors in your astral temple).

Perform the following meditation to find your key. If you find the right key, the image will naturally be the first thing you want to see whenever you enter the temple to perform ascension. Sometimes it will take a few tries before you find the key that works best. You'll know if the key isn't quite right if you find your mind shoving it aside in favor of something better.

Ascending to the Daemonic Plane

The final step in learning ascension is to learn to carry a question or desired outcome into the ascended state with you. This way, you can come out of the ascended state with answers and direction. So, for example, if you enter an ascended state with the desire to learn a personalized incense recipe to work with Asmodeus, you can come out of the ascension with that recipe. You can also discover sigils, Enns, and other important information. Or answers to problems or self-work you are currently performing.

So your first step for this ascension session is to choose something important to you. Something you wish to discover about a Daemon, a rite, or yourself.

Use your key to ascend to the Daemonic Plane. Give the Daemons control of your state and simply follow, watch, and listen to what they're telling you.

Now sometimes you'll find that what you think is important - the Daemons don't agree and they'll tell you something else. It's also perfectly okay to go into ascension with no expectations. The latter allows the Daemons to impart wisdom with you as they see fit and necessary, and they WILL inevitably give you something to chew on. That's just how they are. So going into ascension with no preconceived notions is a wonderful exercise for adepts who are seeking their next area of study or personal growth, but have been unable to find it on their own.

It is often suggested that you do not attempt to practice ascension night after night for months at a time because it can make you feel drained or compromise your health. Sometimes the revelations are so profound you'll need several months break in between sessions to work on the issue or to mull over the experience. Sometimes revelations from ascension aren't clear until several days afterward.

Ascension can be a cumbersome method of divination because of this. If you want instant gratification or an answer right now, you may or may not get it during an ascension session.

Dream Divination & Communication

Astral divination and communication with the Daemonic comes in the form of Ascension, but dream divination is another matter entirely. The dreamscape makes communicating with the Daemonic much more interesting. Dreams with Daemons are often in full color, vivid, and leave a lasting impression long after a seer has awoken. I recommend anyone practicing dream divination keep a journal next to their bed and record all such memorable dream encounters.

Learning to divine and speak with Daemons during sleep does rely heavily on being able to dream walk (aka lucid dreaming), especially if you want to remember what the Daemon(s) had to say.

Dream work relies heavily on the ability to work astrally. Working in the astral temple will strengthen your psychic muscles and will naturally carry over into the astral's more difficult cousin, dream walking. Dream divination and communication is, essentially, the ability to go to the astral at will while in REM sleep and speak to the Daemonic, then waking to remember what you did, and still feeling refreshed and rested. It may sound simple, but it often isn't. Remember that astral work isn't the same thing as just using your imagination. You literally *leave your body* when you are successfully in the astral. I've had students who could dream walk easily but had a hell of a time going into the astral while conscious while others can astral travel at will and have a harder time with dream walking. This is normal. If you can do both easily – you are among a rare few. It takes practice and there are just some days it won't or can't happen. Just try again.

The best curative I can give for strengthening your dream work sessions and, in the very least, increasing your chances for success, is to anoint the temples with an oil consisting of camphor and mint, focusing on leaving the body, making it a point to know exactly what questions you want answered. When you fail, try again. Practice, in this sense, is going to improve your chances of success. There are numerous shamanistic techniques and treatises on this subject. I suggest those who wish to learn speaking with the Daemonic in the dream realm research and practice astral travel and meditation as prerequisites to attempting their first dream walk.

Now on to the common communication uses of dream work. Conversing with the Daemonic Divine doesn't have to involve answering questions about your future. Just like any other form of Daemonic divination, it can be used to discover rituals and pathwork. There are also many additional magickal uses for dream walking and dream divination. As a magician, you will undoubtedly find a million and one uses for this skill.

One of the easiest techniques to learn how to do dream divination is as follows:

First, choose a Daemon you wish to speak with. Place his/her sigil beneath your mattress or under your bed. Drink a full glass of water. Anoint your temple and third eye with an oil made of lavender and mint - lavender to induce sleep, and mint to enhance the senses. You can substitute camphor for mint, or use *Tiger Balm*.

Get comfortable and get into bed. Close your eyes and think about the question(s) you want answered. Basically – go into sleep with a clear goal of what you want to know. Now, think the Daemon's enn. Recite it in your head while imagining his/her seal emblazoned before you in the darkness.

Once you fall asleep, the key is to enter that dream state, take control of the dream, find the Daemon, and ask the questions. Oftentimes you'll find yourself sitting with the Daemon or in the presence of the Daemon. I can't begin to tell you how many dreams I've had involving Ronove (aka Ronwe) and a Starbucks. He didn't look Daemonic either. He looked like a distinguished professor. Daemons within the dream will stand out. Their light will be brighter than any other "character" in the dreamscape.

If you have successfully taken over the dream you should also be able to wake yourself up upon completion of the communication so you can immediately write everything down in your dream journal. Sometimes these dreams will be so vivid or emotionally impactful that they'll hold until morning.

The Rituals of Divination

The following section of the book includes a few basic rituals to help you consecrate, dedicate and charge your divination devices as well as rituals to help construct your divination space or draw a Daemon into yourself. Please note that working within a constructed ritual space is not required for those who have experience. I recommend it for those just starting out. However, no matter how experienced you are, don't get cocky. You can still find yourself imbalanced if you're not careful.

Constructing the Balanced Ritual Space

Yes, this is repetitive and is included in several of my books, but with good reason. This construct is the most balanced of all the ritual space constructs and works well for Daemonic Divination.

When calling the Daemons into your ritual circle, the traditional way to do it is to use the enn, or an invocation of your own devise, and use the ritual dagger or your hand to draw the following in the air in front of you (kind of diagonal to the sky if that makes sense), starting at the arrow and ending at the dot:

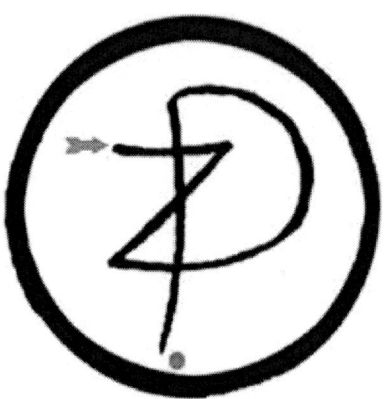

The invocation symbol above is often referred to as the ZD or DZ sigil (because of the shape – not because an actual letter z or d has any significance). It is also used as a sigil representing the all (Satan to some). Within the ZD are nine points representing the nine Daemonic divinities. The nine divinities from the Dukanté Hierarchy are: Satan, Lucifer, Flereous, Leviathan, Belial, Verrine, Amducious, Unsere, and Eurynomous. For the Goetic Hierarchy these points would represent Satan, Oriens, Amaymon, Paymon, Egyn, Adromolech, Astaroth, Belphegor and Lilith. The symbol is one fluid motion and is encircled as a sigil to represent the whole encircling all its parts. The ZD is also employed to invoke each Daemon, no matter which one, with respect to the nine.

Some common courtesies (to avoid disrespect toward the Daemons) when invoking:

- Don't command or be aggressive with the Daemons.
- Don't stab the ritual blade into the air.
- If you are working with Khemetic Daemons like Set, Seshat, Anubis, Thoth, do not use a ritual blade. Instead, use your forefinger and middle finger.
- Do not use a wand, scepter or staff.

The Ritual

Circle construction can be performed in a variety of ways. However, for divination a simple elemental circle construct will often suffice. Yes, you can modify this to invoke divination Daemons like Azlyn, Delepitoré, Ashtaroth/Astaroth, and even Vassago. This creates a balanced ritual space that keeps the practitioner balanced and your Daemonic guests comfortable. It also keeps the space bathed in Daemonic energy, thus keeping the riff-raff from the other side out.

Start at the East point of the circle, draw the DZ in the air with the ritual dagger (without thrusting it) and recite the enn for Lucifer or your equivalent Air Daemon (*Renich Tasa Uberaca Biasa Icar Lucifer*).

Walk to the South point of the circle, draw the DZ in the air and recite the enn for Flereous or your equivalent Fire Daemon (*Ganic Tasa Fubin Flereous*).

West is Leviathan or equivalent water Daemon (or Belial if you prefer Earth West) (*Jedan Tasa Hoet Naca Leviathan*), and North is Belial or equivalent earth Daemon (or Leviathan if you prefer Water North) (*Lirach Tasa Vefa Welhc Belial*).

Then, Satan (*Tasa Raimi Laris Satan*) or the head of your pantheon is invoked from the center.

It is okay to use different elementals. Remember - the entire point of the ritual circle is not for protection, but rather balance and to keep the space rich with Daemonic energy.

This doesn't mean you can't construct different types of circles (or spaces of other shapes) within which to work. Advanced magicians will often find the standard elemental circle too limiting.

Consecration & Dedication of Divination Device(s)

Consecration in this ritual will include a process of cleansing the divination device to clean any unwanted energy from it before we consecrate it and dedicate it to the task of Daemonic divination. By Daemonic Divination, of course, I mean communicating with Daemons exclusively. This will further make it so that nothing but Daemons will want to come through or "use" the device. Daemonic energy is generally too strong for more other types of spiritual entities just as they're often too strong for people for long durations. Therefore other spirits will tend to want to stay away.

For this ritual you will need the following:

- Water
- Salt
- Frankincense (and a charcoal to burn it on)
- One white candle
- Your divination device(s)
- Divination oil (or oil of Daemon you're wanting to dedicate the device(s) to)
- The seal of any Daemons you want to dedicate your device(s) to. I recommend Azlyn, Delepitoré, Astaroth, or Vassago for those of you unfamiliar with Daemons ruling over divination or those of you who are new to Daemonic divination overall. Astaroth is the most helpful and is always willing to work with beginners. Vassago is least friendly to beginners just in case you wondered. But he's still workable. Just harsher. Or you can work with a Daemon you work with often or feel most drawn to.

So first, construct your basic elemental circle as described earlier in this section. Set your divination device(s) on the altar. **Invoke the Daemonic entity you wish to oversee the consecration and dedication.** Mind you that you don't have to dedicate the device to a specific Daemon if you don't want to. You can just dedicate it to the "Daemonic Divine" and ask the Daemons you summon to help you to that end.

Once that particular Daemon is invoked you can begin. Light the candle and incense if you didn't beforehand. Next, hold the divination device up to the flame (don't burn it, obviously) and say, "I cleanse this device in fire that it may bring me rapid sight."

Then sprinkle it with water and say, "I purify this device with water that it may enhance my intuition and bring great wisdom."

Sprinkle it with salt and say, "By salt I make this device pure and bring it great stability."

Then wave it through the incense smoke and say, "By smoke may this device bring great insights and truth."

Hold the device on high and say, "By [Daemonic Name] I consecrate this device to the Daemonic Divine, that nothing but Daemons may communicate with me through it. It is for you and yours alone and no other. Claim it as your own!"

You can leave off that last bit if you are concerned you may only get one particular Daemon from the device. You can modify this to your needs. For example, if you're consecrating and dedicating an earth pendulum, you might invoke an earthy Daemon and say "none but Daemons of earth may communicate with me through this pendulum." You also don't need to say "device". You can insert the proper name of the device(s) into the orations.

Next, anoint the device with the divination or Daemonic oleum of your choice. If you are working with crystals or gazing balls, anoint their stands. If mirrors, anoint them on the back. Then, set the device on top of the Daemonic sigil. At this point you can add on the next ritual – the pillar to charge the item, or you can simply close the rite by thanking the Daemons for coming and telling them to depart in their own time. That choice is yours.

You will likely notice a distinct change in the feel of the device after this ritual.

Charging Your Divination Device(s)

Use this ritual to charge any divination device. As many of you already know, pillar rites are rituals (of various construction) wherein you make pillars of energy within which the object to be charged is encased. It's no different for a divination device. If you want to infuse it with Daemonic energy, a pillar is the fastest way to do that. This is a rather simple ritual that can become a staple in your magickal arsenal.

What you will need for this ritual:

- Five violet or red candles. (You can use yellow if you prefer since yellow is often associated with divination.)
- A knife
- A divination oil or oil of the Daemon you're working with.
- The sigils of the divination Daemon(s) you are seeking to help you charge the device(s).
- The divination device(s)

On the candles, carve the Daemonic sigil(s) and anoint with divination or Daemonic oil. To really personalize this and build on your connection with the Daemons and the device, you can add your blood to the oil. Put the divination device on the center of the altar. Surround it with the five prepared and dressed candles. Invoke the Daemonic force(s) over the candles. Raise and project the energy onto the pillar, imagining its light extending from floor to ceiling running through the candles and the object you are charging. Let the candles burn down completely and then either use the item or start over with new candles and continue charging.

Remember that the candles act as the perimeter of the pillar of energy. Visualizing a pillar of colored light (the same color as your candles) and fast moving energy that extends from the ground to the sky creates the pillar. Usually pillar rites are done for several days up to a month at a time to properly infuse items with the required energies. For divination devices, I recommend at least a week charging before use.

Ritual for Connecting to the Daemonic Divine

There are many different ways of connecting to the Daemonic. The Ascension formulas in the Ascension chapter are a few of those methods. This particular method requires a table.

Within a prepared ritual space (i.e. elemental construct for those unfamiliar with my terminology), invoke the Daemon you wish to contact. You can use an enn or an invocation of your own creation. Simply ask the Daemon if (s)he will come forth and join you that you may speak with him/her.

Set the sigil of this Daemon on the table or space between you. Now close your eyes and take several deep breaths. Begin to chant the Daemonic enn (if you know it). Become aware of your breath and the energy around you. Reach out your hands and place your finger tips on the sigil. Imagine the Daemon sitting across from you, and doing the same. Your fingertips touch. When you feel that touch, take another deep breath and open your eyes. Pull out your divination device and place it on top of the sigil. Begin your divination session.

A Basic Daemonic Divination Ritual to Amplify Results

Anoint your third eye and pulse points with a flying ointment. Construct your ritual space to Azlyn and Ashtaroth (or one of them if you so choose). To do this, simply invoke each Daemon of divination from each of the quarters or points. Sit in the center of the ritual space with your divination device and work as you normally would.

Drawing Down Belial

This is actually a channeling ritual to draw a Daemonic force into you. Unlike a basic connection ritual, it's a drawing down, drawing into you, type ritual. While this particular example is a ritual to Belial, you can use it for ANY Daemonic entity simply by replacing the invocations. If there are other participants – make them stand at the North Quadrant. The medium him/herself should perform the ritual.

Make sure your ritual space is comfortable. At the four quarters invoke Ashtaroth, giving offerings of white or gold candles and incense (two parts myrrh, one part cinnamon, and one part sandalwood) to each quarter as you go. On the North and South Quadrants invoke her with: *Tasa Alora foren Ashtaroth* and on the East and West Quadrants invoke her with: *Serena Alora Ashtaroth Anay*.

Then stand in the center of the ritual space and invoke Belial by employing his enn: *Lirach Tasa Vefa Wehlc Belial*

Go to each of the four quarters and offer him a handful of dirt while chanting his Enn the entire time.

Return to the center of the ritual space. "I draw thee, Belial! I draw you into me that you may use my eyes to see and my lips to speak. Come forth! Arise! Arise!"

Now sit comfortably and allow any participants to now join you at the center of the circle. Close your eyes and begin to recite the enn again. Relax.

You may feel your head fall forward as you fall into the darkness that should be surrounding you now. Feel the Daemonic energy around you and you will feel Belial merging with you, stepping into your body. Take another deep breath. Relax and continue to think the enn. Let your head fall forward. Feel the Daemon enter.

You should feel your body but have no control of your speech. You may hear your voice distantly, know it's your voice, but know it isn't you. The Daemon will stay as long as he has something to say, but once he's finished he will leave and you will be left in control of your faculties and likely rather exhausted.

Please be sure to have gotten plenty of rest and hydration before this ritual and mind your aftercare once the ritual is complete. Take time to balance and ground yourself and get any rest, food, or drink you require after the ritual. The key is to listen to your body.

Additional Daemonic Commentary

I asked the Daemons to share anything additional they would like to add to this book, this section. So here it is. Their commentary on Divination, Ascension, Magick, and whatever else they saw fit to include. I have not censored any responses from any of the Daemons that came forth to share their wisdom for this book. It will speak to each of us as individuals, and my guess is we'll each get from it what we need.

BELIAL

Since this book was named for Belial, I felt it was most fitting that he get the first words in this chapter. He had this to say:

"In the tenebrous splendor of the left hand of darkness, Abaddon dwells in a gnashing of teeth. The pillar of severity stands strong against the oncoming storm that bludgeons the seeker through Da'ath. The master of hosts, of the armies of Gog and Magog, his Majesty Lucifuge stands guard at the gate saying, "Only he who hath understanding can enter here. Here he must unravel the mysteries of the squares in the temples. The Great Beast.

Leviathan, the serpent, Avatar of Yamm. The Destroyer. We return thus to Abaddon before the raging sea where Tiamat beckons us into the darkness. Hail unto Lucifer, Prometheus, Dagon. Your light is the beacon of wisdom."

LUCIFER

I always get a little hint of snarkiness when working with Lucifer. He is both mischievous and wise and I always get a sense that in his attitude we can learn a little something about not taking ourselves too seriously, and taking time to enjoy life – not just analyze it.

"Before you three gates in the shapes most pleasing your eye. Light spills from them resplendent, in the glory and majesty of the Highest on High. Behold, for entering the gate will pull you asunder, drag you through the depths of the abyss. Here I shall pontificate you, my scepter anoints thee and I share with you the wisdom of all time. Of all ways of science and philosophy. I am the light bringer, rising above as the sun, as Ra. My golden wings glide on the wind to lead you to the fruits of knowledge beyond the cloud crossed star-scapes and breath of angels. Now listen well for I shall not waste words or breath on the hubristic magician whose mental acrobatics offend me.

I do here admire those who seek knowledge but not those who worship it. Knowledge is for use eternal, not to be admired for what it is and used as fodder to bloat one's ego. What I say should be marked for edification of the self and masses. What a disastrous plight is the mind trapped in the sphere of the earth. It cannot ascend."

LILITH

"Stand forth and bring with you the edges of the earth. The glades of lavender bring sleep, the world beyond comes in clear focus. We arise from within, in glory bound and freed in thought. Dancing by moonlight swirls the singing trumpets in white. Behold this music of the divine. Arise in yourself, arise and be free. To roam forever in the great unknown darkness drenched in splendid colors. Hail unto you, great serpent deceiver you. For you encompass all things. You."

LEVIATHAN

Within the Mirror seek darkness bound, stretched into the abyss. Beneath the waves and cold of my depths, find wisdom and comfort. There is justice and truth here for those who seek it. I am within the mirror, beneath.

Resources & Reading

The following books may be rather helpful in your further study of Daemonolatry-based Daemonic Divination, Ascension, and Channeling.

For Basic Daemonolatry:
The Complete Book of Daemonolatry – S. Connolly

For Basic Daemonolatry Magick:
Daemonolater's Guide to Daemonic Magick – S. Connolly

For Sigil Divination:
Sigillum Diaboli – S. Connolly

For Daemonolatry Magickal Incenses, Oils & Brews:
Wortcunning for Daemonolatry – S. Connolly

NOTES

NOTES

NOTES

More from DB Publishing & Official Melissa Press

By S. Connolly

- The Complete Book of Demonolatry
- The Daemonolater's Guide to Daemonic Magick
- The Art of Creative Magick
- Daemonolatry Goetia
- Infernal Colopatiron or Abyssal Angels: Redux
- Curses, Hexes & Crossings: A Magician's Guide to Execration Magick
- Honoring Death: The Arte of Daemonolatry Necromancy
- Necromantic Sacraments
- Kasdeya Rite of Ba'al: Blood Rite of the Fifth Satan
- Nuctemeron Gates
- Abyssal Communion & Rite of Imbibement
- Keys of Ocat (currently published by Nephilim Press)

By M. Delaney

- Sanctus Quattuordecim: Daemonolatry Sigil Magick

By E. Purswell

- Goetic Demonolatry

By Martin McGreggor

- Paths to Satan

Various Authors (Compilation Books)

- My Name is Legion: For We Are Many
- Demonolatry Rites
- Ater Votum: Daemonolatry Prayer
- Satanic Clergy Manual
- Ritus Record Libri

Forthcoming from DB Publishing & Official Melissa:

- Wortcunning for Daemonolatry – S. Connolly
- A Witch's Book of Recipes – Brian McKee
- Grimorium Daemonolatrie – S. Connolly & M. Delaney (Melissa)
- Sacrae Infernales – S. Connolly

Workbooks and Journals by S. Connolly

- The Goetia Workbook
- 30 Days of Spirit Work
- The Spirit Workbook
- The Meditation Journal

Lightning Source UK Ltd.
Milton Keynes UK
UKOW03n1433260814

237593UK00002B/10/P